I Want to Go Home

Anxiety and Depression Poetry

Sheena Bennett

Copyright© 2020 by Sheena Bennett

I am writing this book of poems for all the people out there that suffer from Anxiety and Depression. I want you to know you are not alone, even though it feels like it most of the time. There are people that can help you just have to reach out.

If you do not have Anxiety and Depression, after reading this maybe you can understand a little more about someone that does. Not everyone has the same thoughts, these are mine. Be gentle with people. You never know what they are going through. Try to be there for the people in your life that have Anxiety and Depression.

I hate it Here

I want to go Home

Home as in Heaven above

But... I know I can't

There are two reasons why

I feel like I don't belong here

I just want to go home

I love how I do nothing Right

I love how you are never Happy

Everything is my Fault

Everything is always Wrong

We should never talk about it

We should pretend it is alright

There are days I need someone there

Someone, Anyone that will care

All alone in the world I am

No one gives a damn

We don't talk about Depression

That will only lead to rejection

I just needed someone

Before I finally came undone

Dear Self,

    You are stupid. I don't care if they say you are smart. You are not. You can't do anything right. Nothing. Everything you touch falls apart. No one likes you. They make fun of you behind your back. You're ugly, lazy and fat. Get up and do something. You are worthless and pathetic.

    Sincerely,

    Depression

I have hurt for so long

My body, my mind, my soul

It all hurts

All the time

Chemicals out of wack

Anxiety running rampant

Depression yelling in my ear

My mind going and going

What if's and Why's

How long can it possibly keep going?

Please

Please make it STOP

I just wanted a Friend

Someone to talk to

Even if they don't comprehend

A Friend to tell my accomplishments

And failures in life

Someone to give acknowledgement

Why am I different

Why can't I be like you

I am sad and I am tired

I just want to be like you

Happy

    A word I do not know

Happiness

    A feeling I do not feel

Joyful

    An adjective that will never describe me

Depression

    A condition that runs my life

I don't care

I don't care if you like me

    Hell, I don't like myself

I don't care what I look like

    Look at what I am working with, really

I don't care if my life is a mess

    I am a looser anyway

I don't care about tomorrow

    It's going to suck

I don't care

I just wanted to feel better

I just wanted my life together

My mind goes its own way

No matter what my therapist may say

Worksheet and pill and I'm out the door

Nothing helps me anymore

Things will be going ok

Could I have found my way?

A hobby returns as a passion

I can actually feel compassion

Soon the valley of Depression appears

The up and down of my life for years

Darkness creeps into my mind

I know it's coming for me from behind

"Fat Butt"

A small joke

That hurt my soul

From two words

Thoughts of suicide occurred

Something Happens

My mind reacts

My body gets tired

My heart and soul are sad

It can stay this way for some time

Just tired and sad

I stay

I need a Refill

I only have one Pill

I must call; on the phone

Me; all alone

They will answer "Hello"

I will stumble, I know

Deep breath, don't stall

Just press Call

1 and 2 and 3 and 4

Breath In, Breath Out

Live in the Moment

Worrying of the past leads to Depression

Worrying of the future leads to Anxiety

Practice Mindfulness

Meditate

Exercise

Go outside

Imagine the worse situation

Apply that to Everything, Everyday

Is it plausible

No

Is it real to me

Yes

I just want to go to bed

Close my eyes

Not ever get up

Just lay there and dream

Dream of lovely things

For when I wake up

Life sucks

Around me

I see all the Bad

I feel the Negative

I taste the Sour

I smell the Heaviness

I cry tears for myself

I cry tears for you

I am sorry I am this way

I want to get better

But I don't know how

I just want to go home

Why must I stay

Let me be free

Of all the pain

I hurt, inside and out

I just want to go home

Hold me when I cry

Listen even if I don't know what to say

Be there

Just be there

So I know someone cares

Take care of each other. Know you are not alone in this battle. Reach out for help.

Printed in Great Britain
by Amazon